Samuel's Ramblings

Samuel Chuy

Presentation by *BookLeaf Publishing*

Web: www.bookleafpub.com

E-mail: info@bookleafpub.com

ISBN: 9789357212755

First edition 2023

To whoever is reading this

ACKNOWLEDGEMENT

Thanks to everyone who encouraged me to do this. Especially to my dad and mum.

PREFACE

Ranging from acrostic to sensory, get excited. None of the characters resemble real people, or else that would be coincidental. I am been driven to write this book mainly because I just want to have an actual book!

The bear from Brazil.

There was a bear from Brazil,
Who lost in soccer 10-nil,
So he went to Rio hill,
To have 99 years to chill,
By the time the years were finished there was no
bear from Brazil!

Afraid of the cat

The rat was afraid of the cat,
The rat sat on a bat on a cat,
But the bat was afraid of the cat,
Why, because the cat was quite fat,
So they jumped off, just like that.

Number 18

Everyone gather around,
If eighteen is the best number, shout it out loud!
Go- kart number eighteen and more,
Hippo number eighteen that actually roars,
Ten plus eight equals eighteen,
Eighteen cats in a jar full of beans,
Eighteen boxes full of excitements and bores,
Number eighteen, the one you've been waiting for.

Creatures of the Deep

What if I told you there were creatures in the
deep,
Creatures so mysterious no watcher has ever
saw,
Monsters on the ocean floor in such a deep
sleep,
That only rise when the cold winter begins to
thaw,

Fins crackling, scales shifting as dark shapes
awaken,
Fishermen unaware just a few yards away,
The creatures start to stand as the rocky earth
quakens,
A salty wave washes the boat as if the monsters
want a say,

Fishermen cries of the kraken and Loch Ness fill
the air,
As these creatures of the deep start to launch up
into the sky.
Towards unsuspecting town and away from their
watery lair,
Over the countryside and the golden fields of
rye,

Military reports for duty as ten tanks roll over
the hill,
In 1 second all the tanks are destroyed to dust,
On every TV the president begs everyone to
chill,
As the whole army is called on with an urgent
tone,"YOU MUST!"

BANG!BOOM!CRASH!BASH!THRASH!KAB
OOM!
As exactly two hundred thousand three hundred
and forty one machines are brought down,
KABOOM!THRASH!BASH!CRASH!BANG!B
OOM!
As another two hundred thousand fail suspecting
town,

But how can you escape this terror of the deep?
But then again, what if this is just a fake?
Then you wake up and your alarm clock goes
Beep,
No sea monsters coming out of the lake!

Ding Dong

Ding dong,
The clock bongs,
It's time to get to work,

Ding dong,
Orchestra songs,
It's time to get to work,

Ding dong,
The day hasn't been long,
It's time to get to work,

Ding dong,
Your company's wrong,
No time to go to work,

Ding dong,
Join the joyful throng,
No work today, let's go to Nanchong!

In the Ching-Chang-Chong

In the Ching-Chang-Chong when the ducks are
long,
In the Chong-Chang-Ching when the worms like
to sing,
In the Chong-Ching-Chang when dogs have
fangs,
And the fangs are really sharp too.

Oh, in the La-Le-Lu, when the ghosts go boo,
In the Lu-Le-La when the sheep go baa,
In the La-Lu-Le when the ants are under special
care,
And the ants make a real racket too!

Loneliness

When loneliness comes,
The miserable sense invades,
Plunging into your heart,

Abandonment felt,
Like you're alone in the world,
And no hope abounds

Bad Efficiency Restaurant

I am waiting for my food,
I am not in a good mood,
And I am starting to brood,
All the chickens need to be shooed,
And the farmers be sued,
I don't care if I'm rude,
I just want my yummy food,
Food that can be chewed.

The Jungle.

I hear the chirping exotic birds of high above,
I see the tree leaves as delicate as the dove,
I feel the wildness of this very remote place,
I smell the humid air rushing to me in the race,
I taste the freshness of the rain drops dripping on
my face.

Black Death

A hundred years or more have passed,
Since terror roamed the city roads,
Bringing down a thousand more,
Of poor, diseased human souls,

The Black Death, t'was it was,
Brought to a city safe and sound,
Rats crawled out of ships and cargo,
And into unsuspecting town,

Disease erupted all around,
Hundreds died in a single morn,
Carts overflowing with the dead,
The mighty veil of health was torn,

Every evening, every night,
The sound of groans were heard,
And after an eternity,
Disease broke off like a retreating herd,

Now the streets no longer cry,
The son, no longer dying,
But beware, reader; beware, reader,
Disease may come if it keeps trying.

Can you imagine?

Imagine imaginary images,
Mountains of cheese, valleys of cake,
Apples of gold, money on trees,
Go-karts of birds, chocolate seas,
Interesting thoughts that form in your mind,
No one has ever thought of before,
And maybe you can be the first,
To invent near-impossible things,
Igloos of pizza and cars of air,
Oh, the things you can do,
Nothing can stop YOU from imagination.

Life of a Bored Kid

Bbbbbbbbbbbbbbbbboooooooooooooooorrrrrrrrrrr
rrrrrrrreeeeeeeeeeeeeeedddddddddddddddddddd
ddd
Nothing to do in the house, nothing to do
outside,
Mum won't let me bake, Dad won't take me for
a ride,
Just lying on my bed, looking around,
No one I can see, not a sound,
Then I realise I'm all alone,
I panic and fumble for the phone,
No phone in sight, now there's so much to do,
Calling my neighbor and my pet dog too,
Suddenly I see a car coming in,
In such a hurry it knocks over the bin,
Two people emerge with their nervous faces,
I run towards them, my boredom cut with lasers,
Then my dad tells the story, and my joy is cut by
maces,
''I was lost in the jungle' my dad explained,
''With nothing more than a biscuit I was very
afraid,
''I was sure I would die in this remote place,
''But I didn't know my life had begun another
phase,

''Suddenly, a rescue patrol emerged, searching,
'' And I call for them, my heart lurching,
''They see me, and lead me to their jeep,
''While I am laid on a bed, I can't help but take
a peep,
''As I'm driven through, back to my house,
But I say, it's okay Dad,
Compared to my problem, it's not that bad!

Gems

A man emerges from the ash, his clothes caked
with mud,
Sunlight barely reached the dying flower buds,
The man was searching, searching for a treasure,
He had brought nothing, nothing for his leisure,
Finally the man found it, and he started digging
like a dog,
After he had removed a pile of dirt, he moved
aside a log,
A chest of precious stones was revealed, and the
man eagerly snatched it,
Inside was priceless jewels, and he picked them,
bit by bit,
Now he didn't need anything, the man trudged
back home,
What he did not notice was that the gems were
made of foam...

The Day I became a Chicken

I was watching TV, relaxing on the couch,
I was eating snacks out of my lunchbox pouch,
Suddenly an unusual feeling came to me,
And then feathers sprouted for all to see,

I thrashed in worry and shock,
And my sister came over to mock,
Then my legs felt weird and I bent over to look,
I saw chicken legs that my father loves to cook,

My back creaked and my arms stretched,
My friends at school would think this was quite
far-fetched,
I tumbled out of the couch and then my throat
felt sore,
I soon heard why when I began to caw!

Then my head changed form as it began to take
a shape,
My mother would think I was a four-footed ape,
I shouted(or clucked) for my dad to come,
Dad took me away with a cheery hum,

He put me on the chopping board and went for a
knife,

I couldn't let Dad take my innocent life!
Dad returned and lifted the blade,
As I saw my life beginning to fade,

They could have wrote "R.I.P Misunderstood
Chicken."
Instead people only heard KFC's,"it's finger
licking"

Space

Space, as dark as night,
Inspiring galaxies,
In space's quietness,

Supernovas crash,
In the beauty of nature,
Awesome universe.

In the land of Bulgaria

In the land of Bulgaria,
There lived a man with malaria,
He said,"I'm not sick!"
"I'll prove you with a lick!"
And so licked a nearby cat,
Then the cat gave him a scratch,
He hurriedly ran away, bleeding and bruised,
But he cried, "I have nothing to lose!"
So he went away to...

In the land of Malaria

In the land of Malaria,
There lived a man with Bulgaria,
The man said,"I'm so sick!"
"I'll prove you with a lick!"
And so he licked a nearby dog,
And was congratulated by a frog,
He went away, with triumph and success,
He said,"Look, my body is all pest!"
So he went away to the...

Race Cars

Racing down high speed highways,
Amazing everyone who comes to watch,
Creating over-exaggerated puffs of smoke,
Ecstatic drivers waving through the window,
Cars plus a bunch of cool stuff equal these,
A day of awesomeness,
Reaching for the finish line,
Such is the world of race cars